PRIMARY SOURCES OF THE THIRTEEN COLONIES AND THE LOST COLONY ™

A Primary Source History of the Colony of
NEW HAMPSHIRE

FLETCHER HAULLEY

rosen central
Primary Source ™

The Rosen Publishing Group, Inc., New York

To the newest member, Hudson.

Published in 2006 by The Rosen Publishing Group, Inc.
29 East 21st Street, New York, NY 10010

Library of Congress Cataloging-in-Publication Data

Haulley, Fletcher.
A primary source history of the colony of New Hampshire/Fletcher Haulley.—1st ed.
    p. cm.—(Primary sources of the thirteen colonies and the Lost Colony)
Includes bibliographical references and index.
ISBN 1-4042-0429-6 (lib. bdg.)
ISBN 1-4042-0676-0 (pbk. bdg.)
1. New Hampshire—History—Colonial period, ca. 1600–1775—Juvenile literature. 2. New Hampshire—History—Revolution, 1775–1783—Juvenile literature. 3. New Hampshire—History—Colonial period, ca. 1600–1775—Sources—Juvenile literature. 4. New Hampshire—History—Revolution, 1775–1783—Sources—Juvenile literature.
I. Title. II. Series.
F37.H28 2006
974.2'02—dc22

2004029481

Manufactured in the United States of America

On the cover: A 1780 view of the Piscataqua River across from Portsmouth, New Hampshire, by Joseph Frederick Wallet Des Barres.

CONTENTS

INTRODUCTION

New Hampshire may be best known for its state motto: Live Free or Die. This noble philosophy first arose during the time when New Hampshire was one of the thirteen original American colonies ruled by England but seeking independence. The small colony was never the biggest, richest, or most powerful of those thirteen colonies. Because of its small size and population, the colony found itself constantly facing difficult times in its early history. The settlers living on the colony's frontiers constantly faced danger from the local Native Americans, who were often angered by the colonial government's actions and policies.

"Live Free or Die"

New Hampshire also faced the constant bullying and aggression of its fellow colonies. For a hundred years, New Hampshire struggled in the grasp of the Massachusetts Bay Colony, a large and forceful political power sitting on its western border. The Massachusetts Bay Colony believed that New Hampshire was weak and could be easily controlled. It fought for New Hampshire's land until the bitter end.

One of the least populated of the thirteen original colonies, New Hampshire's inhabitants often had to fend for themselves against frightening threats from Native Americans, fellow New England colonists, and harsh nature. The rigors of living in the colony made the people tough and capable of dealing with great adversity. They worked hard for what little they had and would work hard to defend what they gained. This gritty spirit is at the very heart of the colonial history of New Hampshire.

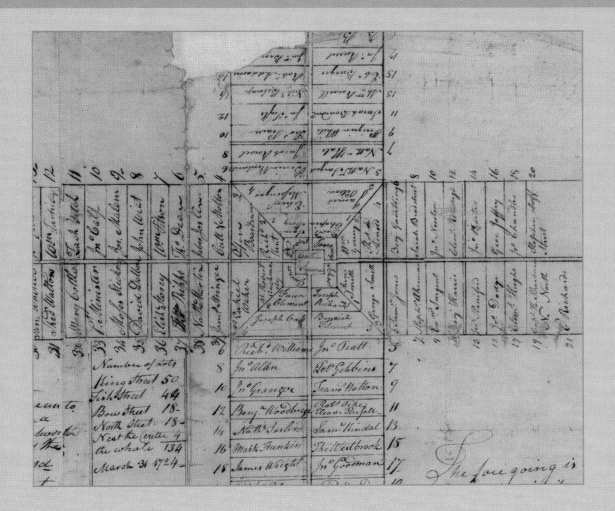

A detail of a circa 1722 lot map for the town of Nottingham, New Hampshire, appears above. A petition for the land upon which the town would be founded was signed on April 21, 1721, by 101 people who mostly came from Boston and Newbury, Massachusetts, and New Hampshire. After the petition was granted, the town's proprietors decided to call it New Boston. When the town's Royal Charter arrived on May 10, 1722, however, it was discovered that the town had been named Nottingham, after Sir Daniel Finch, Earl of Nottingham. The Earl was a close friend of Samuel Shute and Joseph Dudley, governors of Massachusetts. Among the town's original proprietors was Peregrine White, a descendant of a *Mayflower* passenger of the same name. Nottingham's Peregrine White was the first child of English parents to be born in New England. In addition, Benning Wentworth, a future governor of New Hampshire and son of John Wentworth, the lieutenant governor of Massachusetts, was also one of the town's proprietors.

CHAPTER 1

The Birth of New Hampshire

The story of settlement in New Hampshire begins around 12,000 years ago. These earliest residents were Native Americans who, 25,000 years earlier, had crossed a land bridge that once existed between Asia and North America. There is little evidence of these first inhabitants in New Hampshire, and they are not believed to be the ancestors of the Native Americans whom the English and French explorers encountered when they first landed in New England.

In the New Hampshire and Maine area in the 1500s, there was one main group of Native Americans, the Abenakis (which means "the people of the dawn" in the Algonquian language). Those who lived in New Hampshire were called the Sokoki Abenakis (which means "those who were separated from the people of the dawn"). To the west, in Massachusetts, New York, and Vermont, the most powerful Native American group was the Iroquois, a militant and well-organized confederacy of many individual tribes. The various Abenaki tribes never united like the Iroquois did. Instead, they lived seminomadic lives. They would come together in small towns of about 100 residents in the spring and summer to harvest crops and to fish. As winter approached, they would separate into smaller familial clans and move away from the villages to hunt. There was occasional warfare between the Abenakis and their neighbors, but never on a large scale. All in all, the Abenakis led peaceful lives on rich land that produced an abundance of food for them.

John Cabot was born in Genoa. His name in Italian is Giovanni Caboto. Though he was a citizen of Venice, he moved to England in 1495. The following year Cabot received a patent from Henry VII, king of England, to find a direct passage to Asia that would lie farther north than the routes of Christopher Columbus's two earlier expeditions on behalf of England's rival, Spain. This was referred to as the Northwest Passage. With his son Sebastian on board, Cabot sailed the *Matthew* across the Atlantic Ocean in 1497, and landed on the coast of Labrador, or Cape Breton Island, in modern-day Canada. This wood engraving shows John and Sebastian Cabot landing on the coast of North America during their first voyage to the New World.

The Italian explorer John Cabot, sailing on behalf of England, first came to the area in the summer months of 1497. Cabot actually beat Christopher Columbus to the North American mainland by several years since, on his first voyage to the New World, Columbus had landed in the Caribbean islands and returned to Europe before ever reaching the coast of the North American mainland. Cabot is thought to have landed in Labrador, Canada, and stayed for only two days. However, he

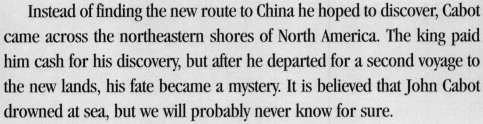

JOHN CABOT

John Cabot was an Italian merchant who had spent most of his life trading in the Middle East. When he heard about the riches brought back from Columbus's voyages to the New World, he decided to find a western route to China. King Henry VII of England gave Cabot the right to explore new lands in 1496. He tried to set sail the same year, but bad weather forced him to return. The next year he finally left on his own voyage westward.

Instead of finding the new route to China he hoped to discover, Cabot came across the northeastern shores of North America. The king paid him cash for his discovery, but after he departed for a second voyage to the new lands, his fate became a mystery. It is believed that John Cabot drowned at sea, but we will probably never know for sure.

immediately recognized the enormous possibilities of these new lands. He returned to England and promptly received more ships and more men to launch a return voyage. Cabot disappears from the history books during this second voyage, but the land he found in the New World does not.

The Abenakis and the Europeans

Once the northeastern coastline of North America had been discovered, it quickly became a beacon to Europeans seeking wealth. Most of the men who journeyed to the New World in these times were fishermen. They sailed to the New World to fish the rich, untouched coastlines of America. They returned promptly to Europe with their catch, rarely spending any time on land.

John Mason, the man to whom the king of England would grant the land that became New Hampshire, described the richness of

This eighteenth-century watercolor by an unknown artist depicts a man and a woman of the Wabanaki Confederacy. The Wabanaki, or Eastern, Confederacy was an alliance of five Algonquian tribes who had joined together to defend against Iroquois attacks. The five tribes, which ranged in territory from New England to Quebec and New Brunswick in Canada, were the Abenaki, the Penobscot, the Maliseet, the Passamaquoddy, and the Mi'kmaq. Each tribe was politically independent, but consulted together on matters of war, peace, and trade. The watercolor shows how interaction with Europeans began to change the traditional lifestyles of the Wabanaki tribes, including New Hampshire's Abanaki population. The woman *(left)* wears a blouse made of European cloth. The couple's hoods are also made of this cloth, while their leggings and moccasins are made of animal skins.

New Hampshire fishing in the 1600s: "May has herrings, equal to 2 of ours, lants and cods in good quantity. June has capline, a fish much resembling smeltes in form and eating, and such abundance dry on shore as to load carts, in some parts pretty store of Salmon, and Cods so thick by the shore that we hardly have been able to row a boat through them," as quoted in John Mason's *A Briefe Discourse of the New-found-land*.

Encounters between the fishermen and the Abenakis were generally peaceful. The Europeans were a curiosity to the Native Americans and possessed trade items they had never seen before. The Native Americans, in turn, created handcrafted goods that aroused much interest in the Old World. Unfortunately, these friendly meetings came with an unknown, and deadly, price for the Abenakis. The Europeans brought with them diseases—such as measles, smallpox, and chicken pox—that the Abenakis had never come in contact with before. Their bodies were unable to fight off the many different sicknesses, and the Native American population in Maine and New Hampshire dropped greatly over the next hundred years.

In 1564, an unknown sickness hit the Abenakis particularly hard. Then, in 1586, an outbreak of typhus (a bacterial disease that causes a high fever and a rash) ravaged the Abenakis. By the early 1600s, there were only 10,000—half the original number—Abenakis in New Hampshire. The Maine Abenakis were hit much harder, with only 5,000 of their once 20,000-strong populace surviving the typhus epidemic.

Contact between the Abenakis and the Europeans expanded when the French and English started to establish trading outposts in the area. They sought the high-quality furs that would fetch extremely high prices in the shops of London and Paris. Most of these trading outposts were located in neighboring Maine or Canada, but their influence extended throughout the territory that would become New Hampshire. The French outposts south of the modern-day Canadian border were short-lived. They were attacked by the English and Native Americans alike and were usually abandoned shortly after being established. As the English and French competed for the natural

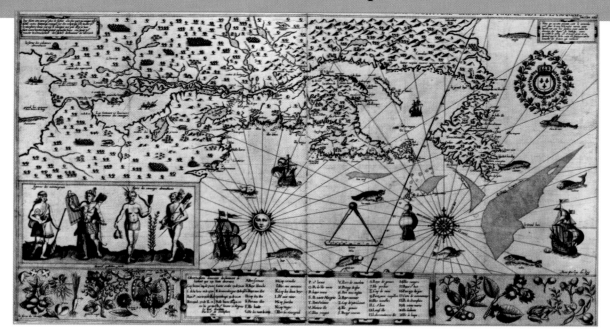

More than sixty years after a failed attempt to establish a French colony in Quebec by Jacques Cartier, King Henri IV of France once again tried to encourage settlement in the area. A small fleet of ships was sent to Acadia, a region that extended from modern-day Nova Scotia to Maine. One of the men on board was Samuel de Champlain, an experienced sailor and soldier. It was his job to chart the coastline of this region from present-day Cape Cod to the Bay of Fundy (in Nova Scotia). In addition to mapping the coastline, Champlain also recorded his observations of vegetation and the area's Native Americans. Champlain's 1612 map of the coast of what would come to be New England includes drawings in its margins of various Native Americans and specimens of plants.

riches of New Hampshire and for control over the New World, their quarrels often turned into outright warfare.

Exploration and Opportunity

Meanwhile, European travelers continued to explore New Hampshire. Martin Pring landed at the future site of Portsmouth in 1603. Famed French explorer Samuel de Champlain mapped the state's coastline in 1605. John Smith, renowned for his leadership efforts in the Jamestown colony and his written accounts of the explorations along the New England coast, sailed New Hampshire's shores while fishing and naming islands in 1614. Smith had initially named the present-day Isles of Shoals after himself—Smyth Isles. He liked the area so much he wrote his friends back in England to tell them about the pleasure and freedom New Hampshire offered and would continue to offer: "Here should be no landlords to rack us with high rents, or extorted fines to consume us. Here every man may be a master of his own labor and land in a short time," as quoted by John Mason.

Back in England, the discovery of the New World had aroused excitement and optimism in a wide range of people. Some saw the potential to make money in the vast and rich new lands. Others saw the opportunity to create new, purified societies free of the oppressive rules, corruption, and religious intolerance of England. The Separatists were a group of Protestant Christians who wanted to cleanse the Church of England of its perceived corruption. King James I had no patience for dissent (or criticism and disagreements) with the country's dominant Anglican church. He jailed many of the group's leaders. Some of those who remained free decided to sail first to Holland, and later in 1620 to New England. There, the Separatists and Puritans would create a utopian, or perfect, society. The Pilgrims' voyage to the New World was that of the famous *Mayflower*, which landed at Plymouth, Massachusetts, in December 1620.

It was about this time that John Mason received a land grant for what would later become the colony—and then the state—of New Hampshire. Mason was not a religious dissenter like the

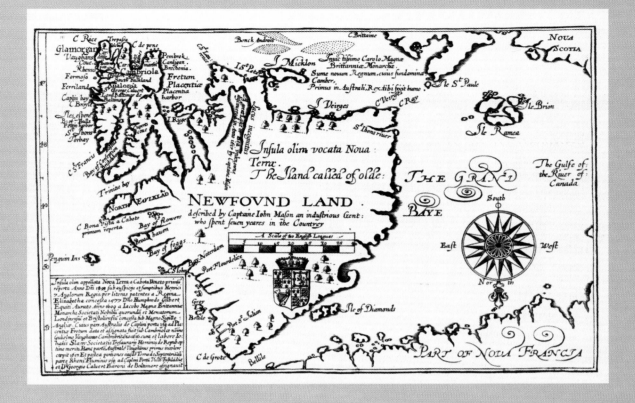

As governor of Newfoundland from 1615 to 1621, John Mason first came into contact with Sir Ferdinando Gorges, a fisheries commissioner in Newfoundland. Together they received land grants to territory in northern New England, which they agreed to divide between them in 1629. In the woodcut at right, Mason and Gorges are seen studying a map of the territory and dividing the land into what would become Maine and New Hampshire. At top is a map of Newfoundland created by Mason.

Pilgrims who landed in Plymouth in 1620 or the Puritans who sailed to Massachusetts Bay in 1629. Rather, he was in the New World to seek fame and fortune. In 1615, Mason was named the governor of Newfoundland in Canada and later returned to England to hold an assortment of different posts with the government. After receiving a land grant in Massachusetts, Mason, along with a man named Ferdinando Gorges, received another grant for what would become New Hampshire and Maine in 1622. Gorges and Mason split the land. Gorges walked away with Maine, and Mason took possession of New Hampshire, which he named after Hampshire, the English county in which he was raised.

CHAPTER 2

John Mason never actually set foot on New Hampshire land after he was granted the territory. For him, the New World was nothing but a moneymaking venture. He parceled out land to men who would move to New Hampshire to establish settlements and trading posts. The first man he sent was David Thomson, a Scot. Thomson established New Hampshire's earliest European settlement at the mouth of the Piscataqua River. This was Little Harbor, located in modern-day Rye. For a short time Little Harbor served as a trading post for furs and fish.

The Early Settlers

Edward Hilton, a merchant from London, was the next European man to establish a settlement in New Hampshire. He founded the town of Dover, a few miles north of Little Harbor, in 1623. Dover became the first permanent settlement in New Hampshire when Little Harbor was abandoned only a few years after it was founded.

Profit and Puritanism in New Hampshire

Seven years later, an English company called the Laconia Company founded the present-day town of Portsmouth under the name of Strawbery Banke. It eventually became the colonial capital and the most important town in New Hampshire. However, Portsmouth's initial settlers faced difficult times. After exploring the nearby forests, the captain of the mission decided that the area would never be profitable, and he sailed back to England. The Laconia Company then cut its ties to the settlement, and the settlers were left to fend for themselves, which they did quite successfully, against all odds. The fort surrounding the town provided its citizens

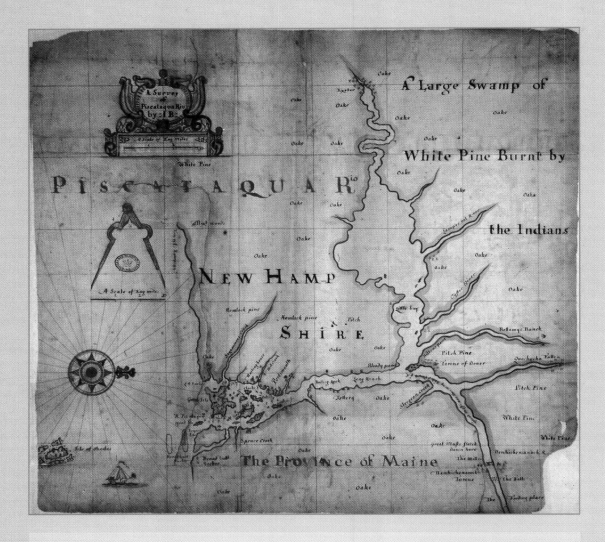

This 1699 map shows both existing and proposed British forts along the Piscataqua River in New Hampshire. John Mason encouraged development along this river as early as 1623, when he sent London fish merchants to the area to establish fishing colonies at the mouth of the Piscataqua. One of these merchants, David Thomson, established New Hampshire's first settlement, Little Harbor or Pannaway (modern-day Rye). A few years later, the other merchant, Edward Hilton, founded a settlement 8 miles (12.9 km) away called Northam (present-day Dover). John Mason died in 1635, just as he was preparing to visit New Hampshire for the first time. He had spent more than £22,000 on his colony to clear the land, build houses, and prepare for its defense. By the time of his death, income from the fur and timber trades had greatly added to that earned from fishing.

John Wheelwright *(right)* studied at Cambridge University in England and became a vicar of the Church of England. After becoming a Puritan, however, he immigrated to Boston and became a pastor of a church in Massachusetts. His sister-in-law Anne Hutchinson angered Puritan leaders by insisting that one's conscience and personal intuition were more important in religious matters than blind obedience to authority. Wheelwright publicly defended Hutchinson's views and was banished from Massachusetts.

John Wheelwright

with a safe place to live. It also drew fur traders and fishermen from all over the region to its busy markets.

In 1638, two disgraced ministers made their way to New Hampshire, each one founding a new town. Reverend John Wheelwright, a Puritan, had left England to escape religious persecution. However, five years after his arrival, he was run out of the Massachusetts Bay Colony for creating religious divisions among his congregation. Having reached New Hampshire, he founded the city of Exeter before he was run out of town again when New Hampshire fell under the rule of the Massachusetts Bay Colony.

Reverend Stephen Bachiler arrived in Boston from England in 1632. His political and religious opinions quickly got him into trouble in the Massachusetts Bay Colony. When Roger Williams, a young, intelligent Massachusetts Puritan, argued against the colony's forced relocation of Native Americans and its strict religious requirements for politicians, he was expelled from the colony. The only man to vote against the expulsion was Bachiler. Bachiler himself was then made to feel as unwelcome as Williams. This disagreement drove him to New Hampshire, where he founded the town of Hampton.

While the Massachusetts Bay Colony was a large, organized, strongly religious colony, New Hampshire was not. What brought people to New Hampshire was its lack of an intrusive religious government. Unlike the Massachusetts Bay Colony, founded and run by Puritan leaders, New Hampshire was a colony founded exclusively for the purpose of making profit. The secular, or nonreligious, nature of its government gave the outcast ministers such as Bachiler and Wheelwright—and all New Hampshire settlers—the freedom to practice their religion in their own way and to express their opinions without fear of punishment or expulsion.

John Mason had died by the time Bachiler and Wheelwright founded their towns. Mason did very little to establish a colonial government or even much of an official presence in New Hampshire. For him, the colony was strictly a business venture. It would be the men who followed him who would fight for New Hampshire's freedom from the bullying dominance first of the Massachusetts Bay Colony, and later of the mother country itself, England.

Life Under Massachusetts Rule

The freedoms that had attracted the religious outcasts and others who were out of step with the rigid rules of Massachusetts would be short-lived. The various New Hampshire towns founded after Mason's land was granted to him were independent of each other, and each had a separate set of laws. In 1639, they voted to unite and form a single government to administer their affairs.

English settlers led by David Thomson arrive on the shores of the Piscataqua River at Odiorne's Point. Here they would found New Hampshire's first settlement, known as Pannaway Plantation, or Little Harbor (present-day Rye). Before long, these settlers would build a stone manor house, a smithy, cooper's workshop, a fort, and fish drying facilities. Thomson's son, John, was the first child born in New Hampshire.

The towns' leaders wrote to the king of England in October 1641 to explain the reasons behind their decision:

> Whereas sundry mischief and inconveniences have befallen us, and more and greater may, in regard of want of Civil Government, his gracious Majesty having settled no order for us, to our knowledge we chose names are underwritten, being inhabitants upon the River of Pascataqua have voluntary

agreed to combine ourselves into a body Politick, that we may the more comfortably enjoy the benefit of his Majesty's laws and do hereby actually engage ourselves to submit to his Royal Majesty's laws. (Courtesy of Yale University Law School's Avalon Project).

New Hampshire had never been provided with a government by Mason or the British crown. This letter proposed that the colonists create their own government in the name of England. At this very same time, however, the Massachusetts Bay Colony claimed the territories of New Hampshire as its own. Massachusetts maintained that New Hampshire lay within the territory given to Massachusetts in its original colonial charter. This claim was later proven to be false, but not before Massachusetts was allowed to rule officially over New Hampshire for nearly forty years.

A disagreement between the people of New Hampshire and the Massachusetts government lasted until the unified New Hampshire towns relented and finally agreed to accept Massachusetts rule in 1641. The towns were still allowed to control "town affairs" and were permitted to send representatives to the Great and General Court at Boston, but control over New Hampshire as a whole became the responsibility of the lieutenant governor of Massachusetts.

The colony was not founded and governed by strict religious leaders, but while it was under Massachusetts rule, it fell under Massachusetts's often harsh laws. Disgruntled Puritan settlers from Massachusetts and other New England colonies began to migrate to New Hampshire in this time period as well, adding more religious influence to the previously business-driven towns.

Life as a colonist in the mid-1600s was difficult. Families labored all day long to raise crops in what was often stony soil

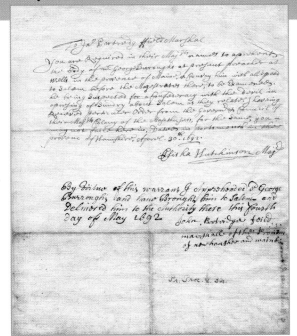

Eunice "Goody" (Goodwife) Cole *(above left)* was the only woman in New Hampshire to be convicted of witchcraft. Some of her fellow townspeople in Hampton claimed to have seen her take on the shape of a dog, cat, and eagle. The devil was said to have taken on the form of a dwarf and sat at her table. In addition, livestock deaths and fatal boating accidents were blamed on Cole. At the age of sixty-four, Cole was convicted, whipped, and sentenced to life imprisonment. She was released after fifteen years, but was later arrested and jailed again for several months. At the age of eighty-eight, she died, and a mob was said to have carried her to a field and driven a stake through her heart. Above right is an arrest warrant for George Burroughs, a man from Maine accused of witchcraft. See transcription on page 54.

and harsh weather conditions. There was little help available if the crops failed and families became desperately hungry. As a result, they took comfort in their religion and often saw life as a stark struggle between the forces of good and evil. Living on remote, isolated farms and in infrequent contact with neighbors, many New Hampshire settlers succumbed to a spirit of distrust and superstition.

In 1656, nearly forty years before the infamous Salem witch trials of 1692, New Hampshire experienced its own hysteria concerning accusations of secret relationships with evil spirits. Whispers about Eunice "Goody" Cole had circulated for years. She was an old, unkempt, and mean-spirited person when she moved to Hampton, and she was said to have only grown worse with age. She lived atop a hill, and her well delivered the best water in the area. She shared it with no one, and the town resented both her good fortune and her selfishness.

Finally, after years of gossip about her, and driven by the townspeople's envy and resentment, town officials charged Goody Cole with witchcraft. She was found guilty and thrown in jail for life. Though Goody Cole wasted away in prison, it was an unusually light punishment for the charges, which generally carried the death penalty. When the town could no longer pay for her upkeep in the Boston jail, Cole was released, only to be charged with witchcraft again in 1673. She was found not guilty this time but lived out the rest of her life in solitude in the same town that had cast her out.

Goody Cole was one of the few women to be convicted of witchcraft in New Hampshire, but there were plenty of others who were charged and eventually let off.

Slavery in New England

Sadly, slavery was an important aspect of colonial American history. Though slavery was far more common in the southern areas of North America, it was still legal and practiced in the north, including in New Hampshire. European traders brought African slaves to the New World for the first time in the early 1500s. Early settlers had tried to use Native Americans as slave labor before this, but

[1]

A

PARTICULAR

OF THE

Royal African Company's

FORTS and CASTLES

IN

AFRICA.

I. CAPE-COAST-CASTLE bought of the former Company.
The Fortifications consist of Outworks, Platforms and Bastions, and has been enlarg'd with new Buildings, and made regular by the present Company, with Bricks, Lime and Tarras, was seven Years a doing, having Apartments for the Director-General, Chaplain, Factors, Writers, Artificers and Soldiers, Magazines, Ware-houses, Store-houses, Granaries, Guard-Rooms; two large Tanks, or Cisterns, built with Brick and Tarras sent from *England*, and holding about two hundred Tons; Repositories to contain one thousand Negroes, and Vaults for Rum; Work-houses for Smiths, Armourers and Carpenters; seventy four great Guns, small Arms, Soldiers-Coats, Blunderbusses, Buccaneer-guns, Pistols, Cartouch-boxes, Swords and Cutlasses, Ammunition for great Guns and small Arms; Stores and Tools for Brick-layers, Brick-makers, Smiths, Carpenters, Coopers, Surgeons, Armourers, Gunners and Gardeners; a compleat Chappel, and a good Library of Books; Pinnaces and Cannoes attending on the Castle and Garrison, and for fetching and carrying Materials for Building, and Stores to and from the Out Factories. This Castle is situate in *Fettur*, the Residence of the Company's General, who manages their Trade and Alliances with the several Kingdoms, and opens a Trade to *Sabo, Cabesterroe, Arcania, Caffero, Dankera* and *Assentee*; and is a Repository of Goods for supply of all the Factories: It has Gardens and Grounds producing all Necessaries for the Factories and Shipping, as Plantanes, Bonanoes, Pine-apples, Potatoes, Yams, Corn, Coleworts, Cabbages, and all other *European* Refreshments: Also Ponds of fresh Water, and the Castle is a security for all Ships in the Road; and by small Vessels taking in Cargoes, and Directions from thence, carry on the Trade to Windward at these several Places, viz. *Cape Mount-Serradi, River Cestos, Sanguinee, Sajo, Cestra Crew, Wappo, Grand Cestra, Cape Palmas, Sabo* on the *Quaqua Coast, Tabow, Petera, Drewin, River Andrea, Red Cliff, Cottrawe, Cape Labow, Jack* and *Jack, Bassam, Assantee, Akanee, Cape-Apolonia*; and to Leeward, as far as the River *Benio*, and old and new *Callabar*; whereby a considerable Trade has been preserved and carried on to the Vending of 60 to 70,000*l. per Ann.* in Goods and Merchandize.

FORT

In 1660, Charles II, king of England, granted the Royal African Company a charter that provided it with a monopoly on trade with West Africa. As part of this trade, the company began supplying captured and kidnapped West Africans as slaves to England's colonies in the New World, including New Hampshire. The document above is a broadside that describes the company's thirteen forts and five factories in West Africa.

found them too difficult to control and searched for alternatives. Africans, uprooted from their nations, families, and land, would be much easier to enslave in the New World.

In the end, about 11 million African slaves were brought to the Americas, though relatively few were forced to work in the North. Because of its rich soil and warm weather, the South became home to plantations (or large farms). These large plantations, operated by wealthy colonial landowners, in turn needed many hands to tend them. Slave labor seemed like an economically logical choice to some American colonists.

The plantation system could never work in the northern colonies, which experienced extreme cold, had a far shorter growing season, and often less fertile soil. Nonetheless, slave labor was still used in parts of the North. The first record of a slave appearing in New Hampshire dates from 1645 in Portsmouth. The few slaves who lived in New Hampshire are noted in the wills and records of some of the more wealthy families. The first accurate recording of New Hampshire's slave population is from 1727, when more than fifty slaves were reported to reside in the colony. Most of these slaves were used by merchants in their businesses and by rich families as household servants. Also in New Hampshire were larger numbers of free blacks who, by most accounts, lived in comparative freedom.

CHAPTER 3

Bloody Warfare on the Frontiers

The period from 1675 to 1700 was a difficult time in New Hampshire for both Europeans and Native Americans. King Philip's War, named after a Native American chief of the Wampanoag (a branch of the Algonquian), began in the fall of 1675. Accounts differ as to the exact causes of the war. But the spark was probably provided by the murder of a Christian Native American who was serving as an informer to the English. Philip may have ordered the murder himself. As a result, three Wampanoags were tried for his murder and executed. This in turn provoked a Wampanoag attack on the village of Swansea in June 1675, followed by other raids. For the most part, King Philip's War seemed to be a spontaneous outburst of hostility born of simmering frustration over white settlers' increasing encroachment on Wampanoag land.

King Philip's War

This wave of raids and counterattacks caused many settlers to move from the frontier back to the relative safety of Boston. In fact, most of Maine was abandoned for the duration of the war. Regardless of exactly what triggered King Philip's War, it was the day-to-day tensions between European settlers and Native Americans that ultimately pushed both sides into violent conflict.

The New England colonies did not take the Native American threat lightly and responded by trying to push the tribes out of southern New England so that larger settlements such as Boston would not be threatened. The fighting in southern New England

PHILIP. *KING* of Mount Hope.

THE
HISTORY
OF
PHILIP'S WAR,
COMMONLY CALLED
THE GREAT INDIAN WAR; OF 1675
AND 1676.
ALSO,
OF THE FRENCH AND INDIAN WARS AT THE EASTWARD,
IN 1689, 1690, 1692, 1696, AND 1704.

By THOMAS CHURCH, Esq.

WITH
NUMEROUS NOTES
TO EXPLAIN THE SITUATION OF THE PLACES OF BATTLES, THE
PARTICULAR GEOGRAPHY OF THE RAVAGED COUNTRY
AND THE LIVES OF THE PRINCIPAL PERSONS
ENGAGED IN THOSE WARS.
ALSO,
AN APPENDIX,
Containing an account of the treatment of the natives by the early voyag-
ers, the settlement of N. England by the forefathers, the Pequot
War, narratives of persons carried into captivity, anecdotes
of the Indians, and the most important late Indian
wars to the time of the Creek War.

BY SAMUEL G. DRAKE.

SECOND EDITION WITH PLATES.

The unexampled achievements of our fathers should not be forgotten.
WASHINGTON.

What wars they wag'd, what seas, what dangers past,
What glorious empire crown'd their toils at last............CAMOENS.

EXETER, N. H.
PUBLISHED BY J. & B. WILLIAMS.
1824

Known to the Puritans as King Philip, Metacom *(above left)* was chief of the Wampanoags, a Native American tribe concentrated in coastal Massachusetts. Devastated by European diseases and frustrated by ongoing Puritan incursions on his land, Metacom began to attack Plymouth Colony villages between Providence, Rhode Island, and Boston. Interestingly, Metacom was the son of former Wampanoag chief Massasoit, who had helped save the Plymouth Puritans from starvation fifty years earlier. This engraving of Metacom was made by the Massachusetts patriot Paul Revere in 1772. The title page of an 1824 history of King Philip's War appears above right.

caused the Abenaki tribes in the area to flee north to their kin in New Hampshire. The New Hampshire Abenaki population increased dramatically, swelling to numbers not seen since before the various epidemics of disease in the late sixteenth century.

After King Philip died, the war between the colonists and the Native Americans continued in northern New England. Settlers in New Hampshire soon found themselves at odds with the newly arrived Native Americans in the area, and the intensity of the war increased again. At long last, the conflict ended in 1676, when Philip was killed. The English colonial government recognized the sovereignty of the Abenaki tribes and agreed to pay them rent for the use of some of their land by white settlers.

In 1685, Edward Randolph was sent by the the new English king, James II, successor to King Charles II, to examine the colonies. He wrote back to the Crown about the causes of King Philip's War:

Various are the reports and conjectures of the causes of the present Indian war . . . Some believe there have been vagrant and Jesuit priests, who have made it their business, for some years past, to go from Sachim to Sachim, to exasperate the Indians against the English and to bring them into a confederacy, and that they were promised supplies from France and other parts to extirpate the English nation out of the continent of America. Others impute the cause to some injuries offered to the Sachim Philip; for he being possessed of a tract of land called Mount Hope, a very fertile, pleasant and rich soil, some English had a mind to dispossess him thereof . . . But the government of the Massachusetts (to give it in their own words) do declare these are the great evils for which God has given the heathen commission to rise against: The woeful breach of the 5th commandment, in contempt of their authority, which is a sin highly provoking to the Lord: For men wearing long hair and periwigs made of women's hair; for women wearing borders of hair and for cutting, curling and laying out the hair, and disguising themselves by following strange fashions in their apparel: For profaneness in the people not frequenting their meetings, and others going away before the blessing be pronounced: For suffering the Quakers to live amongst them and to set up their thresholds by Gods thresholds, contrary to their old laws and resolutions . . . (As quoted in *American History Told by Contemporaries*, Albert Bushnell, editor.)

Randolph's letter reveals the anxious state of mind of the colonists at the time and the degree to which a religious outlook infused the governments of the New England colonies. First, the colonists disagreed about how the war started. Some blamed the English seizure of King Philip's land. Others blamed the recent attempt by French Catholic missionaries to convert the Native Americans and perhaps turn them against the English. The government of Massachusetts claimed that the war was actually a punishment from God for the slack morals of the colonists, including violation of the fifth commandment (Thou shall not kill), men wearing wigs made of women's hair, and women adopting frivolous hairstyles.

In his letter to the king, Randolph goes on to reveal the opinions about Native Americans held by many colonists. The chief concern expressed is for the financial loss of 1,200 houses, 8,000 cattle, and thousands of bushels of crops during the war. The loss of Native American lives are listed right afterward, showing that they were thought to be similar to property. Indeed, Randolph mourns the loss of 3,000 potential laborers

A casualty list from the last major battle of King Philip's War appears at right. The battle took place on June 29, 1677, at Moore's Brook in Scarborough, Maine. The casualty list is dated July 4, 1677, and also records the types of wounds received. Two soldiers from Salem, Massachusetts, John Curwin and John Price, wrote to their commanding officer, Major Daniel Dennison, claiming that thirteen colonists were injured and twenty-three killed. The list seems to be inaccurate, however, because Salem records record nineteen men wounded, while some of those listed as dead by Curwin and Price did in fact survive the battle. See transcription on pages 54–55.

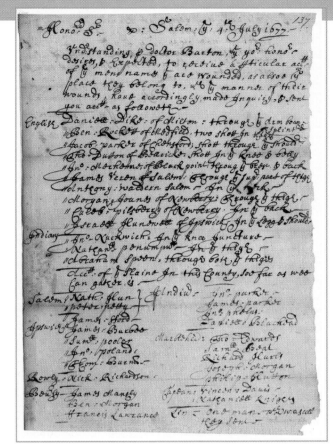

rather than 3,000 individual Native American lives. Given that the English thought of and treated the Native Americans as less than human, it is no wonder that massacres between the two sides were so common. The Native Americans were locked in a life-or-death battle, fighting for their ancestral homelands against an often brutal enemy.

King William's War

The peace following King Philip's War did not last long. Another war, King William's War, broke out in 1689. Unlike the previous war, caused by hostilities between settlers and Native Americans, this war was caused by tensions back in Europe. The new king, James II, had tried to turn England, a Protestant country since 1534, back

On July 1, 1690, the opposing forces of William of Orange, Protestant king of England, and James II, the Catholic and exiled former king, met at the river Boyne, a few miles west of Drogheda in Ireland. James was supported by an army composed of loyal English supporters, Catholic Irish, and some French troops, all united by a desire to see a Catholic return to England's throne. William, in turn, was supported by English and Dutch Protestants and Danish mercenaries. A scene from the ensuing battle appears above. James would be defeated at the Boyne and exiled to France. This was the last major challenge to a Protestant monarchy in England, as William and his wife, Queen Mary, daughter of the defeated James, secured and stabilized their power. This also marked a turning point in Irish history, as the island's Protestant minority, with the backing of the English crown, began to dominate and oppress the Catholic majority.

into a Catholic kingdom. The English people were not ready to accept this, and James II finally fled to France, where the French king protected him. James's daughter, Mary, and her husband, William, both Protestants, took control of the English monarchy.

Louis XIV, the French king, demanded that James be restored as king, but William and Mary and the majority of the English people

This portrait of William and Mary, king and queen of England, may have been created to celebrate their coronation. Mary was the Protestant daughter of Catholic king James II. She was married to her first cousin William, a Dutch prince who was twelve years older than she, in order to strengthen an alliance with the Protestant Netherlands. Despite the fact that this was a politically arranged marriage, they were said to have developed a deep love and respect for each other over time.

refused. As a result, a war erupted in Europe that soon led to war in the New World between the French and English colonies. The French and English in North America had lived in relative peace until this point, but their differences were far greater than their similarities. The English colonies were Protestant, while the French colonies were Catholic. The two religions had yet to learn how to live together in peace and mutual respect. Perhaps more important, each side was also envious of the other's fisheries and trading outposts. As a result, both sides were eager for war when the word came from Europe that the time had come.

Native American allies were recruited by both the French and English colonies to help fight their war. The Abenakis sided with the French, their longtime trading partner in the North, while the Iroquois nation in the west sided with the English. In New England, the Iroquois attacked French colonists, who responded by attacking Seneca Indians (one of the six tribes of the Iroquois Confederacy). When the French crossed through the northern part of New York's territory, the English turned the Iroquois war party loose in the summer of 1688. They struck French settlements deep into Canada, even sacking Le Chine, a town only a few miles from the French colonial capital of Montreal.

The Abenakis were motivated to join the war when the English reneged on several promises agreed to at the conclusion of King Philip's War. For example, English cattle frequently got into Native American crops and ruined them by grazing and stamping them down. Settlers also netted rivers used by Abenaki tribes, cutting off their supply of fish. Aside from these provocations, the Abenakis were encouraged to attack the English by their French allies, who wanted to inflict harm on the English colonies without having to use their own troops.

After diplomacy with the English colonists failed, the Abenakis' next move was to strike at Dover, New Hampshire, in June 1689. Two Native American women begged the town's major for a place to stay until morning. They were granted permission to enter the town. Then, in the dead of night, they threw open the town's gates to a raiding party waiting just outside. Dover was destroyed. Of the fifty people living there, half were killed, while the other half were taken captive and carried off to French territories. The major who had let the two women into the town was tortured to death.

In 1694, the English garrison at Oyster River, in New Hampshire, became the next victim of the war. A Native American party led by a French commander named Villieu was headed to Boston for a planned attack. Confronting the onset of a harsh New England winter and dwindling food supplies, however, they decided to cut their journey short and attack at Oyster River instead. Half of the settlement was burned to the ground, and the war party killed or captured about 100 of the town's 300

Queen Anne's War was the American offshoot of the War of the Spanish Succession fought between France and England between 1702 to 1713. In North America, British and French forces, with their Native American allies, attacked each other's settlements in Nova Scotia, Newfoundland, Massachusetts, and elsewhere in New England and throughout the North American colonies. Queen Anne's War ended when the Treaty of Utrecht was signed in Europe in 1713. At right is a treaty signed by representatives of Massachusetts and New Hampshire and "the Eastern Tribes" of Native Americans who had been allied with the French during the war. See transcription on pages 55–56.

inhabitants. The Oyster River raid was intended to strike in Boston, at the heart of England's power in the New World, but instead it degenerated into mass murder. King William's War continued like this for another three years. Each massacre led to reprisals and further massacres.

Finally, after eight years of often brutal warfare, a peace agreement was reached in 1697 between France and England. James, the exiled Catholic king of England, died a few years later. Other European conflicts would provide new causes for new wars in the years to come. In the end, little was changed in New Hampshire or greater New England. All territory seized by either the French or English was given back when the peace treaty was signed. Only the memories of brutal frontier massacres by colonial settlers and Native Americans alike remained.

CHAPTER 4

The Wentworth Dynasty

Massachusetts's official control of New Hampshire would last until 1679, when it would become an independent royal province. However, Charles II never followed through on fully securing New Hampshire's freedom from Massachusetts. New Hampshire was again placed under outside control with England's creation of the Dominion of New England in 1688. New Hampshire was again separated from Massachusetts in 1691, but it shared a governor with its more powerful neighbor until 1741. In that same year, numerous recurring disagreements over the colonies' borders were finally resolved by King George II of England.

Land Disputes

New Hampshire grew slowly compared to the other American colonies. Since the entire land had been deeded to John Mason, his heirs made life difficult for those who tried to move onto and settle parts of the territory, even many years after Mason's death. Mason's heirs tried to lay claim to land that was already in use by many settlers. The heirs of Mason sued the settlers in court, and the cases dragged on for years. The messy legal situation made few settlers want to move to the colony if they could not be guaranteed ownership of the land they settled.

The problems were not resolved until 1749, when the Mason heirs finally reached a settlement with which they were happy. In the wake of the settlement, the new availability of land drew people into the colony for its hunting, fishing, and mining opportunities. One of New Hampshire's greatest resources—its

Though a Massachusetts official, Lieutenant Governor John Wentworth was a New Hampshire resident and was determined to protect the colony's interests against its larger and often overbearing neighbor to the south. During his term of office, Massachusetts claimed large stretches of New Hampshire's territory. By stressing his colony's loyalty to both the throne and the Church of England, Wentworth was able to persuade King George II to resolve the boundary disputes in New Hampshire's favor.

lumber—was declared off-limits to private businesspeople by the king of England, who claimed the colony's high quality lumber in the name of His Majesty's Navy. Over time, however, a thriving black market for New Hampshire lumber arose.

New Hampshire's Independence and the Beginning of the Wentworth Dynasty

Massachusetts Bay Colony lieutenant governor John Wentworth took over control of New Hampshire in 1717, beginning a three-generation dynasty of Wentworths in New Hampshire politics. Wentworth was solely responsible for winning New Hampshire's freedom from Massachusetts. Wentworth may have been an employee of the Massachusetts Bay Colony, but he lived in New Hampshire and was a devoted New Hampshirite.

In 1719, a group of Scotch-Irish immigrants founded a town they named Londonderry, after the Irish city from which they came. They had left Ireland's northern province of Ulster to escape religious conflict and economic hardship. These immigrants immediately began using the skills they had learned and practiced in Ireland in their new home in New Hampshire. In Ireland, they had been flax farmers and weavers. From the flax, they were able to make linen goods. New World flax was of a much higher quality than the flax used in Europe, so European nations began to import American flax. Indeed, many of the Irish who came to America were transported in the empty hulls of barges that were on their way back to the New World to pick up more flax for the European market.

The traditional, high-quality methods these Irish and Scottish weavers used made their linens famous throughout the world. By 1750, Londonderry town officials had to appoint inspectors to stamp all Londonderry linen, since other linen manufacturers elsewhere were using the city's name in an attempt to profit from its good reputation. Such was the fame and quality of Londonderry linen.

Starting in 1720, Massachusetts started to lay claim to large amounts of New Hampshire's western border. Wentworth appealed to England for a resolution of the conflict, depicting New Hampshire as a small, bullied province that was extremely loyal to the king and devoutly Protestant. King George II ruled in favor of Wentworth and New Hampshire in 1740, and all of the land taken by Massachusetts was returned. This decision marked the end of Massachusetts's rule of New Hampshire, and the next year New Hampshire was appointed its first governor.

Benning Wentworth, the son of John Wentworth, was born in Portsmouth, New Hampshire, where he also died at the age of seventy-four. In 1741, Benning Wentworth became the first royal governor of New Hampshire. Following King George II's settling of the border dispute between Massachusetts and New Hampshire, New Hampshire finally gained independence from the neighboring colony and its own governor. Before becoming governor, Wentworth was a merchant who shipped timber, livestock, and provisions to the colonies of the Caribbean.

When the king appointed the first governor of New Hampshire, he did not look far beyond John Wentworth. Benning Wentworth, John's son, was the king's choice. As governor, Benning continued his father's work of separating New Hampshire from Massachusetts. A regional rivalry between the people even started at this time, with the New Hampshirites mocking the blue-blooded, aristocratic ways of the Massachusetts Bay Colony. New Hampshirites enjoyed the independent course that Benning followed during his twenty-five years in office, which helped give their colony a distinct and individual identity.

Ethan Allen and the Green Mountain Boys

Benning Wentworth encouraged settlers to move to New Hampshire by selling off massive land grants in the area that eventually became the state of Vermont. This policy caused friction with neighboring New York, which claimed that it actually owned the land that Wentworth was handing out. However, 140 townships were drawn up and distributed by Wentworth before New York was able to present its case to the Crown. In 1765, King George III resolved the case, giving the land to New York.

The governor of New York then demanded that the thousands of settlers living on the land pay for it a second time. The settlers refused. When the governor sent officers to evict them, the settlers took up arms. Ethan Allen, a man who would later become famous for his role in the American Revolution (1775–1783), organized them in 1770 into a militia called the Green Mountain Boys. They chose their name after the New York governor had threatened to push them back "into the Green Mountains" (in present-day Vermont) if they did not vacate their land. Allen was a charismatic leader and organized a well-armed, die-hard militia.

The New York authorities did not dare to venture into Allen's territory, and the Green Mountain Boys operated as both the government and law enforcement of the region. In this way, they held off the much-hated "Yorkers" until the American Revolution began. When the revolution came, Ethan Allen was caught by British forces during a poorly planned attack on well-fortified Montreal. He was released in exchange for British prisoners of war and advocated Vermont's independence from both New York and New Hampshire when he returned.

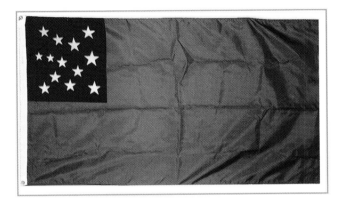

Ethan Allen *(above left)* was born in Connecticut but moved to New Hampshire at the age of twenty-eight to trap and explore in the backwoods. He settled in the area that was part of the New Hampshire Grants (also known as the Benning Wentworth Grants). This territory included 131 towns west of the Connecticut River that actually belonged to New York and, after a long dispute, eventually became the state of Vermont in 1790. A citizens' militia called the Green Mountain Boys was formed in 1770 to protect the New Hampshire grants from New York's attempts to seize them. Allen was the militia's colonel-commandant. The militia also fought in the Revolutionary War and captured Fort Ticonderoga from the British in 1775. Above right is a replica of the militia flag that the Green Mountain Boys carried with them into battle.

Benning Wentworth died in 1770. He was a generally well-liked and highly respected governor, yet he had been forced to resign his office after dismissing New Hampshire's Assembly during the Stamp Act crisis of 1765. His nephew, Sir John Wentworth, succeeded him as governor. Sir John Wentworth was the last of the New Hampshire royal governors. The

Dartmouth College *(above)* was founded by Eleazar Wheelock in 1769. Wheelock was a minister who had earlier established the Moor's Charity School in Lebanon, Connecticut. This school was devoted to the education of Native Americans. Hoping to turn the school into a college, Wheelock relocated to Hanover, New Hampshire, and established Dartmouth. Royal Governor John Wentworth gave Wheelock the land upon which the college would be built, and King George III gave the college a royal charter. This charter created a college "for the education and instruction of Youth of the Indian Tribes in this Land . . . and also of English Youth and any others." Dartmouth is named for William Legge, the second Earl of Dartmouth, a financial supporter of Wheelock's educational efforts.

American Revolution cut his term six years short after he gained the post, yet he was an able leader and was well liked by the people. He built roads, created a colonial militia, ordered the first accurate map of the royal province, and was instrumental in the founding of Dartmouth College (now one of the nation's eight Ivy League universities).

Sir John Wentworth and the Onset of Revolution

The American Revolution was caused mainly by increasingly heavy taxation placed upon the American colonies without any corresponding colonial representation in the British parliament. Colonists, especially those of the merchant class, began to desire greater freedom from the mother country and fewer controls over colonial trade. By the mid-eighteenth century, the colonies had become very profitable. Between 1700 and 1770, the amount of money the colonies made each year rose from £500,000 to nearly £3,000,000.

While the colonies were generating income, the English continued to fight very expensive wars with the French over territorial control of North America (wars in which colonists were expected to fight on behalf of the British crown). The last of these ended in 1763, giving the British uncontested control of the land. Though flush with victory, Britain was now deep in war debt, and the colonies were expected to offset the costs. In this way, the colonists were forced to fight the wars on the ground and then pay for the costs of the war effort in the form of heavy taxes.

As tensions between the colonists and Britain over taxation continued to grow and the American Revolution neared, Sir John Wentworth did everything he could to address the colonists' grievances and head off trouble with the mother country. He worked tirelessly with his cousin, the Marquis of Rockingham, a powerful man in British government, to repeal the extremely unpopular Stamp Act. The Stamp Act, a tax on all paper products sold in the New World, outraged the colonists, who had been subjected to a growing number of taxes by the

British parliament. They were tired of being taxed by the British, who would not allow them political representation in Parliament despite their status as British citizens.

Once the British parliament realized what an uproar the Stamp Tax had caused, the tax was repealed on the advice of the various colonial governments. The British government claimed it did not want unnecessary taxes to stifle the economies of the colonies, but in reality the repeal was an attempt to calm the colonists' growing spirit of rebelliousness. It would prove to be too little too late, however. The march to revolution had already begun.

Sir John Wentworth was a lifelong New Hampshirite, and his family had lived in the area for five generations. Still, he was a very loyal British subject and fled the province when the revolution started. He escaped to Canada, which remained loyal to Great Britain. He probably believed that the problems between Britain and its American colonies would be resolved, and he would be able to return to his homeland at some point. He never got that chance, however. After he was made governor of Nova Scotia, Canada, Wentworth died in England in 1820.

CHAPTER 5

New Hampshire and the American Revolution

New Hampshire's role in the revolution was important even though none of the war's battles was fought on the colony's soil. Indeed, New Hampshire became the first colony to declare its independence from the Crown. When Governor John Wentworth fled the colony in fear of his life, Portsmouth became the first of the thirteen colonial capitals to be free of official British presence. Portsmouth went from being the most loyal of cities while the Wentworths ruled and did business there to becoming a major center of revolutionary activity. Two warships were built in the Portsmouth Harbor by local merchants and donated to the revolutionary effort.

John Langdon

Several significant leaders of the revolution hailed from New Hampshire. Some of them, like John Langdon, were wealthy merchants who stood to benefit greatly from the colonies' freedom from England. If the colonies were able to gain their freedom, such merchants would be able to trade freely with any country and escape the trade restrictions and high taxes with which England was saddling the colonies.

Langdon, whose family had been among the initial settlers of Portsmouth, applied his business skills to the revolution by organizing the supplying of the Continental navy. He also personally financed much of the state militia. Langdon represented New Hampshire at the Second Continental Congress in 1775, which led to the drafting and publication of the Declaration of Independence. In 1787, several years after the end of the revolution, Langdon again represented New Hampshire as a delegate to the Constitutional Convention that resulted in the U.S. Constitution and our present system of federal government. Perhaps reflecting New Hampshire's long and troubled history with its powerful neighbor Massachusetts, Langdon vigorously supported a large, strong federal government that would be able to protect smaller states from the larger, wealthier, more powerful states.

Paul Revere and the Raid on Fort William and Mary

Three months before his famous ride through New England, warning of the British arrival, Paul Revere rode to New Hampshire to warn the patriots there that British marines were coming and to protect the weapons and ammunition stored at Fort William and Mary in Portsmouth Harbor. The British never arrived, but the New Hampshire militia was not willing to take any risks because it needed the fort's arsenal. Differing accounts claim that the patriots were led by either John Langdon or Ethan Allen. In any case, the patriots raided the fort on December 14, 1774, lowered the British flag, and made away with the fort's supply of gunpowder.

The next day, thousands of men were rumored to have descended on the fort, carrying away the guns and cannons. These same weapons were used throughout the revolution against the British. The raid on Fort William and Mary was the first organized attack on the British in the name of the revolution.

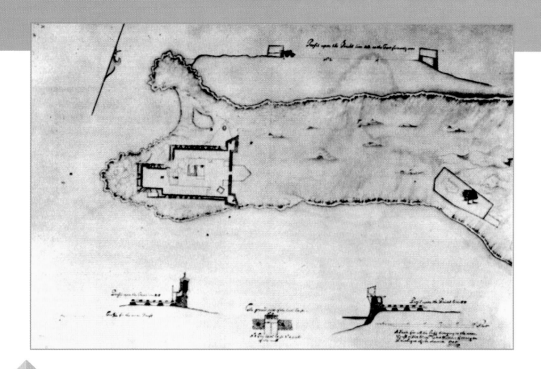

An aerial view of Fort William and Mary appears in this 1705 site plan. Initially known as "The Castle," a fortified defense was first built on Great Island at the mouth of Portsmouth Harbor in 1631. In 1692, the fort was renamed to honor England's new king and queen. The fort had four large cannons until the time of King William's War when, in an attempt to defend Portsmouth from the French fleet, the fort was expanded to allow for nineteen cannons. Stone walls were built around the fort in 1705. In the 1750s, still more guns were added. Despite the growing number of cannons at Fort William and Mary, only about four to eight people staffed it at most times. During periods of warfare or increased tension, however, twenty to forty soldiers might occupy the fort.

However, open hostilities did not break out until after Revere's next ride, warning of the arrival of British soldiers and the battles of Lexington and Concord that followed in April 1775.

The New Hampshire Militia and the Battle of Bunker Hill

New Hampshire produced an important militia that would fight in several of the war's major battles. In June 1775, New Hampshire's troops fought in the Battle of Bunker Hill. The troops from New

Hampshire outnumbered the troops from Massachusetts and Connecticut despite the fact that the battle took place in Massachusetts. The British landed on the shores of Boston Bay expecting to encounter inexperienced and easily frightened rebels. They planned a frontal assault, hoping the rebels would flee at the first sign of danger and aggression. They could not have been more wrong, suffering heavy losses for their brashness.

As the British soldiers neared the rebel lines, the firmly resolute patriots shot them down in a hail of bullets. The soldiers from New Hampshire fired until they ran out of ammunition. They then tried firing nails before finally resorting to throwing rocks at the British. They did not retreat until the last possible moment and suffered only minor losses. The British, meanwhile, had lost a thousand men in the ill-conceived attack.

John Stark

John Stark, the man who led the New Hampshire troops at Bunker Hill, is another interesting example of the different types of leaders the colony produced. Unlike John Langdon, Stark was not a rich man likely to profit from the war. Instead, he was a lifetime soldier. As a lieutenant in Rogers' Rangers (a colonial militia formed by New Hampshirite Robert Rogers) during the French and Indian War of 1754 to 1763, he had already been exposed to British troops who underestimated the colonial militia. Stark happily left the British army after the war. His resentment toward the British grew over the next decade as he watched the passage of the Stamp Act and the Tea Act, and the Boston Massacre of 1770, in which five colonists were shot dead by British troops after a crowd had taunted a British sentry.

On August 16, 1777, General John Stark *(inset)* and his New Hampshire soldiers successfully beat back two waves of British attacks at Bennington. It was a decisive victory that greatly weakened General Burgoyne's army and led to his defeat at Saratoga and surrender two months later. Burgoyne can be seen above, mounted on his horse and organizing a retreat following the defeat at Bennington.

Early on, Stark supported the goals of the revolution and was soon attached to George Washington's Continental army. When he was passed over for promotion in favor of a much less qualified man, however, Stark left the army. The colony of New Hampshire pleaded with him to become the New Hampshire militia's brigadier general—the post he had been passed over for in the Continental army. Stark accepted on one condition: he would answer only to the state of New Hampshire, not to Washington's

The delegates of the united colonies of New Hampshire, &c.
to the inhabitants of the said colonies.

There seems no reason now to expect an accommodation of the dispute between Great Britain and these colonies. All overtures towards it on our part have been ineffectual; and on the other hand no terms have been offered to us, but obedience to unconstitutional authority is required. Arms must decide, whether we shall be subject to laws made by men who are not appointed approved of or controulable by us, whose interest it is to oppress us, and whose pride and resentment will be gratified by humbling us; or shall be subject to laws made by men we ourselves choose and may change, who bear their just proportions of the burthens they impose upon the community, and whose true glory it is to advance its prosperity: in other words, whether we shall resign ourselves to the government of arbitrary rulers, and our property to the disposition of those who are under many temptations, but no restraint to take it away from us, or reserve so much of our natural liberty as permits the doing of every thing but what we ought not, what good men desire not, to do, and may dispose of our property for such public uses, and in such manner and measure as we judge fit. If the enemy conquer, we must be wretched; if not we may be happy; in either event, our posterity must be involved in our fate. Uniting firmly, resolving wisely, and acting vigorously, it is morally certain, we cannot be subdued. Those among us, if there be any, who will not join with us, it is hoped, are as contemptible for their numbers as for their baseness of soul. This is the season when others may prove that love for their country which they profess themselves to be inspired with, and shew that they are what they would appear to be. There are none of us who cannot do some good service in this great conflict. The aged may supply their want of strength by counsel. The young will probably never meet with another opportunity to signalize their

Josiah Bartlett *(right)*, a physician, was a member of New Hampshire's Committee of Correspondence and its first Provincial Congress, both of which came into being after the royal governor John Wentworth disbanded the colonial assembly in 1774 as a result of growing rebelliousness in the colony. That same year, Bartlett was elected to the Continental Congress. He stubbornly insisted on serving as one of New Hampshire's delegates to the Congress despite the fact that Loyalists burned his house down. As a delegate, Bartlett cowrote the July 6, 1775, letter *(left)* from New Hampshire's congressional delegates to the colony's citizens declaring the likelihood of war with Britain as the only remaining way to gain independence and freedom from tyranny. See transcription on page 56.

army. Stark resisted the authority of the generals of the Continental army but obeyed an order from the New Hampshire legislature in the summer of 1777 to march his troops to the town of Bennington, in what would later become Vermont. There, his forces routed the well-trained, heavily armed British. The Battle of Bennington on August 17, 1777, was one of the turning points of the war. It led to the Battle of Saratoga on October 17, 1777, in which a large contingent of the British army was forced to surrender. The loss at Saratoga reinvigorated the Continental army and colonial militias, and caused more and more people in England to stop supporting the war.

In many ways, John Stark—who coined the phrase "live free or die"—embodied the colonial New Hampshire spirit. He was patriotic but independent-minded, idealistic but practical, committed to the revolutionary ideals of freedom and fairness for all but also self-interested and proud. Stark and his fellow New Hampshirites would draw on these qualities first to fight fiercely for independence from Britain, and then to argue with equal passion and conviction for a new nation that would protect the rights of the few against those of the strong and many.

CHAPTER 6

New Hampshire After the Revolution

After the revolution, New Hampshire's leadership was repeatedly recognized and sought out by the other newly independent American states. New Hampshire representatives cast the ninth and deciding vote at the Continental Congress, ratifying the new nation's constitution in 1788. Franklin Pierce, a native son of New Hampshire, was elected president of the United States in 1853. Pierce was not able to accomplish much of importance while in office, however. He tried to avoid the controversial slavery question that was dividing the northern and southern states as the Civil War (1861–1865) drew near. Unlike Pierce, New Hampshire took a strong stand on the slavery question and fiercely supported the North in the Civil War and sent many of its citizens to join the Union army.

After the Civil War, manufacturing became the state's main industry in the second half of the nineteenth century. Textiles were especially important for the economy. Thanks to the high-quality wood harvested in New Hampshire's lush forests, the lumber industry was another important and lucrative state industry.

Today, New Hampshire continues to be one of the most independent-minded of the states, often advocating the importance of states' rights over federal laws it feels are intrusive. The state is also one of the lowest-taxed states in the Union. As a result, New Hampshire has lured high-tech firms away from heavier-taxed areas in the region such as Boston. However, New Hampshire's natural beauty is its biggest industry and asset. Tourism has become New Hampshire's biggest source of revenue, since the land offers outdoor activities all year round—from hiking, camping, and mountain biking to autumn foliage viewing, skiing, and ice fishing. Every four years, New Hampshire grabs center stage in the political arena as the first state to hold a presidential primary (the political parties' first step toward selecting presidential candidates). The outcome of the New Hampshire primary often influences the rest of the country's votes, and it is generally considered to be one of the most important days in a candidate's campaign.

From humble beginnings as a trading outpost and haven for religious exiles, New Hampshire struggled to grow while enduring constant threats from Native American and French war parties and fending off the controlling grasp of Massachusetts. Despite these difficult beginnings, however, the colony produced some of the finest, most influential leaders of the American Revolution. The fierce independence exhibited by the colony and its people continues to be embodied by New Hampshire, a state that enjoys enduring political influence and a hard-won spirit of patriotism.

TIMELINE

1497 — John Cabot explores the Atlantic Northeast.

Early 1500s — First encounters between the Abenaki Native Americans and European fishermen.

1586 — Typhus decimates the Abenaki population in New Hampshire.

1603–1613 — Martin Pring, Samuel de Champlain, and John Smith further explore New Hampshire.

1622 — The land of what would become New Hampshire and Maine is granted to John Mason by the English crown.

1630 — Portsmouth, originally named Strawbery Banke, is established and becomes the center of trading in New Hampshire.

1639 — The independent settlements of New Hampshire decide to organize a colonial government.

1641 — The Massachusetts Bay Colony, beginning a century of rule over its smaller neighbor, annexes New Hampshire.

1675–1676 — King Philip's War, a war between New England settlers and local Native Americans, takes place.

1689–1697 — King William's War, a war between the English, French, and various Native American tribes, lasts eight years, some of the bloodiest in New Hampshire history.

1717 — John Wentworth becomes lieutenant governor of the Massachusetts Bay Colony, thereby also giving him control of New Hampshire in 1724.

1741 — Benning Wentworth becomes the first governor of the Royal Province of New Hampshire, now fully independent of Massachusetts.

1770–1775 — Ethan Allen and his Green Mountain Boys take up arms to defend their land in western New Hampshire against the colonial government of New York. The land they defend will become the state of Vermont after the American Revolution.

December 14–15 1774 — A New Hampshire militia captures Fort William and Mary in Portsmouth Harbor. This is the first organized colonial attack against the British.

1775 — The third Wentworth to govern New Hampshire, Sir John, flees the colony.

July 4, 1776 — Delegates from New Hampshire are the first to sign the Declaration of Independence.

PRIMARY SOURCE TRANSCRIPTIONS

Page 21: The April 30, 1692, Arrest Warrant of George Burroughs

Transcription and Translation into modern English
To John Partridge, Field Marshal
You are required in their Majesties' name to arrest Mr. George Burroughs, currently a preacher at Wells, Maine, and bring him as quickly as possible to the magistrates in Salem for questioning. He is suspected of devil worship and harming several Salem residents. I have received a particular order from the governor and council of their Majesties' Colony of Massachusetts that you must not fail in this duty. Signed and dated in Portsmouth, New Hampshire, April 30, 1692.

[signed] Elisha Hutchinson, Major

[In a different handwriting] By order of this warrant, I arrested George Burroughs and have brought him to Salem and delivered him to the authorities today, May 4, 1692.

[signed] John Partridge, Field Marshal of the Province of New Hampshire and Maine

Page 29: A casualty list dated July 4, 1677, pertaining to the battle at Moore's Brook, in Scarborough, Maine, on June 29, the last major battle of King Philip's War. Compiled by John Curwin and John Price and sent to their commanding officer, Major Daniel Dennison.

Transcription and Translation into modern English
Honored Sir,
Doctor Barton tells me that your honor would like and expects to receive a full report of the names of the wounded men, their place of residence, and the nature of their wounds. I have investigated and send you the following account:

English
Daniel Dike of Milton: Splintered arm bone
Ben Rockett of Medfield: Two bullets in the thigh
Jacob Parker of Chensford: Shot through the shoulder

Thomas Dutton of Bellricke: Shot in the knee and belly
John Mechenne of Blackpoint: [Shot] through the chest and back
James Veren of Salem: [Shot] through the upper thigh
Anthony Waldern of SAlem: [Shot] in the neck
Morgan Joanes of Newberry: [Shot] through the thigh
Caleb Pilsberry of Newberry: [Shot] in the back
Israell Hunewell of Ipswich: [Shot] in the leg and shoulder

Indians
John Nuckwich: [Shot] in the knee
Nathaniel Penumpum: [Shot] in the thigh
Abraham Speen: [Shot] through both thighs

Page 33: The Portsmouth Indian Treaty of July 13, 1713

Transcription

At Portsmouth, in Her Majesty's Province of New Hampshire, in New England,
the twelvth day of July, in the thirteenth year of the Reign of our Sovereign Lady
Anne, by the Grace of God, of Great Britain, France, and Ireland, Queen,
Defender of the Faith, & c.

Whereas for some years last past we have made a breach of our fidelity and loyalty
to the Crowns of Great Britain, and have made open rebellion against Her
Majesty's subjects, the English inhabitants in the Massachusetts, New Hampshire,
and other of her Majesty's territories in New England, and being now sensible of
the myseries which We and our people are reduced thereunto thereby, we whose
names are here subscribed, being delegates of all the Indians belonging to
Norrigawake, Narrakamegock, Amascontoog, Pigwocket, Penecook, and to all other
Indian plantations situated on the Rivers of St. Johns, Penobscot, Kenybeck,
Amascogon, Saco, and Merimack, and all other Indian plantations lying between
the said Rivers of St. Johns and Merrimack, parts of Her Majesty's Provinces of the
Massachusetts Bay and New Hampshire, within Her Majesty's Sovereignty, having
made application to his Excellency, Joseph Dudley, Esq., Captain General and
Governor in Chief in and over the said Provinces, that the troubles which we have
unhappily raised or occasioned against Her Majesty's subjects, the English, and
ourselves, may cease and have an end, and that we may enjoy Her Majesty's grace
and favor, and each of us respectively, for ourselves and in the name and with the
free consent of all the Indians belonging to the several rivers and places aforesaid,
and all other Indians within the said Provinces of the Massachusetts Bay and New

Hampshire, hereby acknowledging ourselves the lawfull subjects of our Sovereign Lady, Queen Anne, and promising our hearty subjection and obedience unto the Crown of Great Britain, doe solemnly covenant, promise, and agree to and with the said Joseph Dudley, Esq., Governor, and all such as shall hereafter be in the place of Captain, General and Governor in Chief of the aforesaid Provinces or territories on Her Majesty's behalf, in manner following. That is to say:

That at all times forever, from and after the date of these presents, we will cease and forebear all acts of hostility toward all the subjects of the Crown of Great Britain, and not to offer the least hurt or violence to them or any of them in their persons or estates, but will honor, forward, hold, and maintain a firm and constant amity and friendship with all the English, and will not entertain any treasonable conspiracy with any other nation to their disturbance.

Page 48: Letter from New Hampshire Continental Congress delegates to New Hampshire citizens, July 6, 1775:

Transcription
The delegates of the united colonies of New [H]ampshire, etc., to the inhabitants of the said colonies.

There seems no reason now to expect an accommodation of the dispute between Great Britain and these colonies. All overtures towards it on our part have been ineffectual; and on the other hand no terms have been offered to us, but obedience to unconstitutional authority is required. Arms must decide, whether we shall be subject to laws made by men who are not appointed, approved of, or controllable by us, whose interest it is to oppress us, and whose pride and resentment will be gratified by humbling us; or shall be subject to laws made by men we ourselves choose and may change who bear their just proportions of [burdens] they impose upon the community, and whose true glory it is it is to advance its prosperity . . . If the enemy conquer, we must be wretched; if not, we may be happy . . . Uniting firmly, resolving wisely, and acting vigorously, it is morally certain, we cannot be subdued. Those among us, if there be any, who will not join with us, it is hoped, are as contemptible for their numbers as for their baseness of soul. This is the season when others may prove that love for their country which they profess themselves to be inspired with, and show that they are what they would appear to be. There are none of us who cannot do some good service in this great conflict . . .

GLOSSARY

charter A written contract; a guarantee of rights and privileges granted by the ruling power of a state or country.

colony A body of people living in a new territory that is governed by a parent state.

constitution The basic principles and laws of a nation or state that detail the government's powers and duties and the rights of citizens.

declaration An official statement of principles.

delegate A person chosen as a representative for a group.

flax A crop that can be used to make linen.

frontier The lands at the edges of the colonies' borders, far from the major colonial settlements. Frontier settlers often had to fend for themselves without the assistance and protection of a community, militia, or law enforcement.

land grant Territory in the New World often given to wealthy Europeans by kings.

loyalist A colonist who remained loyal to the king of England and wished to remain under British rule.

militia A local group of armed citizens serving during times of emergency.

monarchy A system of government based upon the rule of a king or queen. The right to rule is determined by heritage, rather than elections or appointments.

New England The northeastern part of the United States, from Connecticut in the south to Maine in the north.

New World The land "discovered" by fifteenth- and sixteenth-century European explorers in North and South America.

Old World All of the land in Europe, Asia, and Africa that was known to Europeans before the discovery of North and South America.

outposts Small settlements created by European traders in North America. The Europeans traded iron tools, wool blankets, colorful cloth, guns, knives, and pots and pans with Native Americans in exchange for furs (mainly beaver pelts).

Parliament The British legislature; the part of the government that passes laws in Great Britain.

patriot An active supporter of the American Revolution.

Protestant A member of any of several Christian denominations that deny the authority of the pope and support the Reformation principles first put forth by sixteenth-century religious leaders, such as Martin Luther and John Calvin, who broke away from the Catholic Church.

Puritans Devout Protestant Christians who believed that the Church of England was corrupt and ungodly.

Reformation The religious reform movement that began in the early sixteenth century, when many people began to question the beliefs and practices of the Catholic Church.

repeal To take back, or cancel, a law.

royal province A colony established by the Crown, having its own local government that is wholly independent of other colonies.

FOR MORE INFORMATION

Museum of New Hampshire History
The Hamel Center
6 Eagle Square
Concord, NH 03301-4923
(603) 228-6688
Web site: http://www.nhhistory.org

New Hampshire Division Of Historical Resources
State of New Hampshire, Department of Cultural Resources
19 Pillsbury Street, 2nd floor
Concord, NH 03301-2043
(603) 271-3483
Web site: http://www.nh.gov/nhdhr

New Hampshire Historical Society
The Tuck Library
30 Park Street
Concord, NH 03301-6384
(603) 228-6688
Web site: http://www.nhhistory.org

Web Sites

Due to the changing nature of Internet links, the Rosen Publishing Group, Inc., has developed an online list of Web sites related to the subject of this book. This site is updated regularly. Please use this link to access the list:

http://www.rosenlinks.com/pstc/neha

FOR FURTHER READING

Brown, Jerald, and Donna Belle Garvin. *The Years of the Life of Samuel Lane, 1718–1806: A New Hampshire Man and His World.* Lebanon, NH: University Press of New England, 2000.

Buckey, Sarah Masters. *Enemy in the Fort.* Middleton, WI: American Girl, 2001.

Caduto, Michael J. *A Time Before New Hampshire: The Story of a Land and Native Peoples.* Lebanon, NH: University Press of New England, 2003.

Calloway, Colin, ed. *North Country Captives: Selected Narratives of Indian Captivity from Vermont to New Hampshire.* Lebanon, NH: University Press of New England, 1992.

Davis, Kevin. *The New Hampshire Colony.* Chanhassen, MN: Child's World, 2003.

Fradin, Dennis. *The New Hampshire Colony.* New York, NY: Children's Press, 1992.

Italia, Bob. *New Hampshire Colony.* Edina, MN: Checkerboard Books, 2001.

Piotrowski, Thaddeus. *The Indian Heritage of New Hampshire and Northern New England.* Jefferson, NC: McFarland and Company, 2002.

Shannon, Terry Miller. *New Hampshire.* New York, NY: Children's Press, 2002.

Shaw, Lisa. *New Hampshire Vs. Vermont: Sibling Rivalry Between the Two States.* Grafton, NH: Williams Hill Pub, 1997.

Thompson, Kathleen. *New Hampshire.* Minneapolis, MN: Sagebrush, 1999.

BIBLIOGRAPHY

"The Combinations of the Inhabitants Upon the Piscataqua River for Government, 1641." The Avalon Project at Yale Law School, 2003. Retrieved February 2005 (http://www. yale.edu/lawweb/avalon/states/nh07.htm)

"Edward Randolph's Description of King Philip's War" (1685). Retrieved February 2005 (http://www.swarthmore.edu/socsci/bdorsey1/41docs/45-ran.html).

Elson, Henry William. "New Hampshire," in *History of the USA*. New York, NY: the MacMillan Company, 1904. Retrieved October 2004 (http://www.usahistory.info/New-England/New-Hampshire.html).

Hall, David D. *Witch-Hunting in Seventeenth-Century New England.* 2nd Ed. Boston, MA: Northeastern University Press, 1999.

Karlsen, Carol F. *The Devil in the Shape of a Woman.* New York, NY: Vintage Books, 1987.

Mason, John. *A Briefe Discourse of the New-Found-Land* (1620). Retrieved February 2005 (http://www.mun.ca./rels/hrollmann/relsoc/text/mason.html).

Online Highways. "Ethan Allen, 1738–1789." U-S-History.com. Retrieved October 2004 (http://www.u-s-history.com/pages/ h1271.html).

Robinson, J. Dennis. "Why John Smith Never Came Back." November 18, 1999. Retrieved October 2004 (http://seacoastnh.com/arts/please111899.html).

SHG Resources. "New Hampshire: A General History of the State." 2003. Retrieved October 2004 (http://www.shgresources.com/nh/history).

State of New Hampshire Manual for the General Court 1977. Concord, NH: New Hampshire Department of State, 1977.

"Stephen Bachiler Biography." Biography Base. Undated. Retrieved October 2004 (http://www.biographybase.com/biography/Bachiler_Stephen.html).

Zinn, Howard. *A People's History of the United States*. New York, NY: HarperCollins Publishers, 2001.

PRIMARY SOURCE IMAGE LIST

Page 5: A circa 1722 plan of the town of Nottingham, New Hampshire, signed by town clerk Thomas Bartlett. Housed in the New Hampshire Historical Society, Concord, New Hampshire.

Page 9: An eighteenth-century watercolor by an unknown artist of a Wabanaki man and woman. Housed in the City of Montreal Records Management and Archives, Montreal, Quebec, Canada.

Page 11: A 1612 map of America that first appeared in an account of Samuel de Champlain's voyages along the New England coast, published in 1613. Housed in the Hulton Archive.

Page 16: A 1699 map of existing and proposed colonial forts along the Piscataqua River in New Hampshire. Housed in the Public Record Office, in London, England.

Page 21 (right): An April 30, 1692, arrest warrant issued by the Governor and Council of the colony of Massachusetts for George Burroughs of Wells, Maine, who was suspected of witchcraft. The warrant was written to the field marshal of New Hampshire and Maine, John Partridge, who signed the warrant after the arrest of Burroughs on May 4, 1692. Housed in the Massachusetts Historical Society, Boston, Massachusetts.

Page 23: A circa 1698 broadside entitled "A Particular of the Royal African Company's Forts and Castles in Africa." Housed in the Printed Ephemera Collection, Rare Book and Special Collections Division, of the Library of Congress, Washington, D.C.

Page 26 (left): A 1772 engraving by Paul Revere depicting King Philip, or Metacom. It appeared in the book *The Entertaining History of King Philip's War*, by Thomas Church.

Page 26 (right): A revised edition of a history of King Philip's War written by Thomas Church, entitled *The History of Philip's War, Commonly Called the Great Indian War*, of 1675 and 1676. This 1824 edition includes a new Appendix by Samuel G. Drake, and was published by J. & B. Williams in Exeter, New Hampshire. Housed in the Pocumtuck Valley Memorial Association, in Deerfield, Massachusetts.

Page 29: A casualty list dated July 4, 1677, pertaining to the battle at Moore's Brook, in Scarborough, Maine, on June 29, the last major battle of King Philip's War. Two soldiers from Salem, Massachusetts, John Curwin and John Price, compiled the list and sent it to their commanding officer, Major Daniel Dennison. Housed in the Massachusetts Archives.

Page 31: A late eighteenth-century portrait of William and Mary, king and queen of England, possibly commemorating their coronation. Taken from the *Guild Book of the Barber Surgeons of York*. Housed in the British Library, London, England.

Page 33: A treaty between formerly French-allied New England Native American tribes and representatives of Massachusetts and New Hampshire following Queen Anne's War. It was signed at Portsmouth, New Hampshire, on July 13, 1713, with a later addendum signed at the same location on July 28, 1714. Housed in the Manuscript Division of the Library of Congress, Washington, D.C.

Page 35: An 1870 copy of a 1760 oil portrait of Lt. Governor John Wentworth by Joseph Blackburn. Housed in the New Hampshire State House, Concord, New Hampshire.

Page 37: A nineteenth-century copy of a 1760 oil portrait of Benning Wentworth. Housed in the New Hampshire State House, Concord, New Hampshire.

Page 40: An 1819 painting of Dartmouth College in Hanover, New Hampshire. Housed in the Hulton Archive.

Page 45: A 1705 site plan of Fort William and Mary. Housed in the New Hampshire Historical Society.

Page 47: A circa late-1770s painting entitled *The Battle of Bennington*.

Page 47 (inset): A circa 1780 portrait engraving of John Stark.

Page 48 (left): A July 6, 1775, letter from New Hampshire delegates of the Continental Congress to New Hampshire citizens concerning the likely prospect of war with England. Housed in the Library of Congress, Washington, D.C.

Page 48 (right): An 1873 copy of an original eighteenth century oil portrait of Josiah Bartlett painted by Jonathan Trumbull. Housed in the New Hampshire State House, Concord, New Hampshire.

INDEX

About the Author

Fletcher Haulley has a BA in History from New York University. He is a keen student of American history, politics, and government. Haulley is the author of several previous books, including *The Department of Homeland Security* and *The Help America Vote Act of 2002*. He has also edited an anthology of 9/11 writings entitled *Critical Perspectives on 9/11*.

Photo Credits

Cover, p. 7 Library of Congress, Prints and Photographs Division; pp. 1, 17 © Northwind Picture Archives; pp. 5, 13 (bottom), 21 (left), 35, 37, 48 (right) New Hampshire Historical Society; p. 9 City of Montreal, Records Management and Archives, records group BM7, S2, SS1; pp. 11, 19, 30, 40 © Getty Images; p. 13 (top) Courtesy of the Centre for Newfoundland Studies, Memorial University Libraries; p. 16 HIP/Art Resource; p. 21 (right) Courtesy of Massachusetts Historical Society; p. 23 Library of Congress, Broadside Printed Ephemera Collection, Rare Book and Special Collections Division; pp. 26 (left), 39 (left), 47 (inset) © Bettmann/Corbis; p. 26 (right) © Pocumtuck Valley Memorial Association, Deerfield Massachusetts; p. 29 Courtesy of the Massachusetts Archives; p. 31 © HIP/Scala/Art Resource, NY; p. 33 Library of Congress, John J. McDonough and Janice E. Ruth, Manuscript Division; p. 39 (right) © Rosen Publishing; p. 47 © Corbis; p. 48 (left) The Thomas Jefferson Papers, Library of Congress, Manuscript Division.

Editor: John Kemmerer; Photo Researcher: Hilary Arnold